Famous Explorers™

Amerigo Vespucci

Jeff
Donaldson-Forbes

The Rosen Publishing Group's
PowerKids Press™
New York

To Collin and Emma Fulton

Published in 2002 by The Rosen Publishing Group, Inc.
29 East 21st Street, New York, NY 10010

First Edition

Book Design: Maria E. Melendez and Felicity Erwin
Project Editors: Jennifer Landau, Jason Moring, Jennifer Quasha

Donaldson-Forbes, Jeff.
Amerigo Vespucci / Jeff Donaldson-Forbes.— 1st ed.
     p. cm. — (Famous explorers)
Includes bibliographical references and index.
ISBN 0—8239—5833—7 (lib. bdg.)
1. Vespucci, Amerigo, 1451—1512—Juvenile literature. 2. Explorers—America-Biography—Juvenile literature. 3. Explorers—Spain—Biography—Juvenile literature. 4. Explorers—Portugal—Biography—Juvenile literature. 5. America—Discovery and exploration—Spanish—Juvenile literature. 6. America—Discovery and exploration—Portuguese—Juvenile literature. 7. South America—Discovery and exploration—Spanish-Juvenile literature. [1. Vespucci, Amerigo 1451—1512. 2. Explorers.] I. Title. II. Series.
E125.V5 D66 2002
970.01'6'092—dc21

                                                                    00—012390

Manufactured in the United States of America

Contents

1 Beautiful Florence 5

2 Vespucci the Student 6

3 Vespucci in Spain 9

4 Vespucci's First Voyage? 10

5 An Expedition for the King 13

6 Exploring Venezuela 14

7 Meeting the Native Americans 17

8 Working for Portugal 18

9 A New Continent 21

10 Vespucci's Final Years 22

Glossary 23

Index 24

Web Sites 24

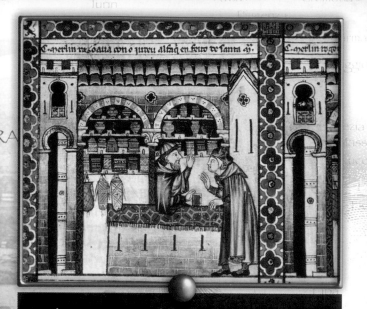

Florence was filled with merchants from all over Europe who traded fabrics and spices.

Amerigo Vespucci is shown holding a map.

Florence

VATICAN ⭐ Rome
CITY

FLORENTIA

During the fifteenth and sixteenth centuries, the city of Florence was one of the wealthiest places in all of Europe. It was also considered among the most beautiful.

Beautiful Florence

Amerigo Vespucci was born sometime between 1451 and 1454 in Florence, Italy. Italy had not yet become a **unified** country, and Florence was a **city-state**. During Vespucci's childhood, Florence was an exciting place to live. Florence, located on the banks of the Arno River, had ships with goods sailing to and from the city. The city was part of a **trade route** that allowed Europeans to buy spices, beautiful fabrics, and gold from India and China. **Merchants** in Florence had to buy these goods from the Turks, who controlled the land between Europe and Asia. The Turks did not allow Europeans to travel safely through Turkish country. Europeans traveling to Asia by land often were attacked and were robbed by Turks. The Europeans wanted to find an ocean route to Asia to avoid land battles with the Turks.

Vespucci the Student

Vespucci's father, Nastagio, believed that education was very important. Vespucci studied Latin, mathematics, literature, geography, and astronomy. Vespucci especially enjoyed studying maps of the world and tracing the voyages of famous **navigators**. He learned to use the **astrolabe** and the **quadrant**, tools used by navigators to map the position of stars and planets. In his early twenties, Vespucci went to work as secretary to his uncle Guido. Guido worked for the Medici family, the family that ruled Florence. Guido was Florence's **ambassador** to France. He took Vespucci with him to Paris, where they lived and worked for two years. Vespucci returned to Florence in 1480 and

Above: This is a fifteenth-century painting of Lorenzo de' Medici, a member of the richest, most powerful family in Florence.

in 1483 went to work again with the Medici family. The Medicis trusted Vespucci because of his work with his uncle Guido. Vespucci was very successful in handling the Medicis' business.

Astrolabe

Quadrant

The astrolabe (above right) and the quadrant (right) were ancient instruments that could measure the position of stars and that were used for navigation.

This is a drawing of the Golden Tower of Seville, a wealthy trading town much like Florence.

This is Port Cadiz, where many ships set sail in search of new trade routes.

This is a map showing the routes of Christopher Columbus's expeditions. Columbus believed he had found the ocean route to Asia. Instead, he landed on islands in the Caribbean Sea.

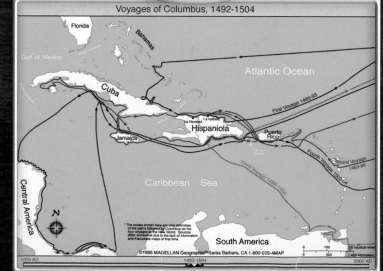

Voyages of Columbus, 1492-1504

Florida

Bahamas

Gulf of Mexico

Atlantic Ocean

Cuba

First Voyage 1492-93

La Navidad   La Isabela

Hispaniola

Jamaica

Puerto Rico

Fourth Voyage 1502-04

Third Voyage 1498-1500

Second Voyage 1493-96

Central America

Caribbean   Sea

N

South America

* The routes shown here are only estimates of the paths followed by Columbus on his four voyages to the New World. Sources differ somewhat due to the lack of information and inaccurate maps of that time

©1996 MAGELLAN Geographix℠ Santa Barbara, CA 1-800-929-4MAP

100   200 nautical miles

100   200   400 kilometers

1000 AD   1492-1504   2000 AD

Vespucci in Spain

In 1491, Vespucci traveled to Seville, Spain, on a business trip for the Medicis. Like Florence, Seville was built on the banks of a large river. Merchants in Seville bought and sold goods from all over the world. Vespucci, using his business contacts with the Medicis, began working as a merchant in Seville. He helped sailors prepare ships for their journeys. In the nearby town of Cadiz, many ships were setting sail in search of a new ocean route to Asia. In 1492, the Italian explorer Christopher Columbus led his first **expedition** west across the Atlantic Ocean. After he landed, Columbus believed that he was in the Indies, the islands near India. In fact, he had found some of the islands in the Caribbean Ocean. Columbus returned to Spain thinking that he had found the ocean route to Asia.

Above: Christopher Columbus was one of the most successful early explorers. He inspired many expeditions to the Americas.

Vespucci's First Voyage?

Columbus became a hero when he returned to Spain in 1493. He was made the governor of the islands he had claimed for Spain. Still, not everyone believed that he had reached India. He did not bring back the treasures that other explorers had found in India or China. The native people he called Indians did not look like Asian people. Vespucci didn't think that Columbus had discovered the ocean route to India. He longed to lead an expedition of his own. Vespucci believed that his skills in map reading and charting the stars would make him a successful navigator. Some historians now believe that Vespucci did lead a trip that sailed from Cadiz in 1497. The

Above: This painting of Vespucci shows him charting the stars. Right: This is a map of the world as people imagined it looked in 1526.

only record of this journey is a letter that Vespucci wrote to a business contact in Florence. It suggests that he sailed into the Gulf of Mexico and traveled along the southern and eastern coasts of today's United States. Vespucci returned to Spain in 1498.

An Expedition for the King

King Ferdinand V of Spain was disappointed in Columbus's second and third expeditions. Columbus had not found much gold or other treasures to bring back to Spain. Settlers living on the island of Hispaniola, a Spanish colony, also said Columbus was doing a bad job as governor. They were **rebelling** against him. King Ferdinand V ordered a four-ship expedition to sail to Hispaniola to check on the Spanish settlers and explore the area further. King Ferdinand V asked Vespucci to **pilot** one of the ships. During the journey, Vespucci spent nights charting the positions of the stars. He saw new, strange **constellations**, or groups of stars, as the expedition moved slowly from the North **Hemisphere** into the South Hemisphere.

Top Left: Ferdinand V sent many expeditions to the Americas. Bottom Left: This is a map of the Western and Eastern Hemispheres. The line through the middle divides the Northern and Southern Hemispheres.

Exploring Venezuela

After one month at sea, Vespucci's expedition reached the coast of today's Brazil. Vespucci knew that the boats had crossed south of the **equator**. He and his men believed that if they sailed farther south, they would reach India. They continued to sail along the Brazilian coast, but nothing looked like India. Vespucci ordered the ships to turn and sail north again. During this time, he created a system that allowed him to chart correctly his **latitude**, or position from north to south, and his **longitude**, or position from east to west. This system helped Vespucci make the first maps of what we now call South America. The beauty of the land reminded him of Venice, a city in Italy. He named the new land Venezuela, which means Little Venice.

Above: This is a painting of Amerigo Vespucci as an old man.
Right: This map shows routes of two of Vespucci's voyages.
Inset: This is a map of South America from 1547.

14

CUBA

HAITI
DOMINICAN REPUBLIC
(Hispaniola)

VENEZUELA

BRAZIL

ARGENTINA

RIO DE
JANEIRO

RIO DE
LA PLATA

PORTUGAL   SPAIN
Lisbon   Cadiz

Dakar

Meeting the Native Americans

s the expedition continued along the Venezuelan coast, the Spaniards met many Native Americans. Using sign language to speak, the Spaniards traded goods such as small mirrors and other metal objects with the Native Americans. The Native Americans were not always friendly. To protect their land, they sometimes attacked the Spanish. Many Native Americans were killed by Vespucci's men and others were forced to return to Spain as slaves. When Vespucci and his crew ran low on food and supplies, they sailed to Hispaniola to restock and to rest. After two months of rest on Hispaniola, the expedition sailed for Spain. Vespucci reached home sometime between June and September in 1500.

Above: This is a painting of an Algonquin Indian from 1585.
 Left: This painting shows a battle between attacking Spanish explorers and Native Americans. Battles broke out among the two groups as the Spanish took the land by force.

Working for Portugal

AMERIGO VESPUCCI

espucci became sick after he returned to Spain. He was too sick to lead another expedition for King Ferdinand V and Spain. As Vespucci recovered from his illness, he received word that King Manuel of Portugal wanted him to lead an expedition. It was not unusual for explorers to work for different nations. Vespucci agreed to lead the expedition for Portugal and to help the Portuguese find an ocean route to India. In May 1501, the expedition sailed from Lisbon, Portugal. Vespucci sailed south to the town of Dakar, on Africa's western coast, for the ship to be loaded with supplies. Vespucci met with members of another Portuguese expedition that was just returning from India. Vespucci paid close attention to the

Above: Vespucci grew famous for his successful expeditions and maps and was honored with statues of himself, such as the one above. Right: This is a painting of Vespucci's voyage in 1501.

details of their trip. Using their travel time and what he knew from his maps of the world, Vespucci was able to figure out the **circumference** of Earth. It was much larger than anyone had ever thought. Vespucci then knew that the countries he had explored were not the Indies.

A New Continent

In the summer of 1501, Vespucci's expedition sailed southwest from Dakar. That fall, he began mapping the southern coast of South America. During the trip, Vespucci and his crew encountered more Native Americans. At times Vespucci went ashore and lived with them, learning their language and customs. Vespucci came to realize that he and his men were not in Asia. Instead, he believed, they were on a **continent** that lay between Europe and Asia. As Vespucci came close to reaching the tip of South America, he and his crew encountered a terrible storm. They were forced to sail northeast to escape it. After a brief stay in Africa, Vespucci's expedition returned to Lisbon, Portugal, in September 1502.

Top Left: This is a picture of caravels, sixteenth-century sailing ships.
Bottom Left: Vespucci spent part of his time in 1501 meeting with many Native Americans on the coast of South America.

Vespucci's Final Years

Vespucci's report about the new continent surprised the entire world. King Ferdinand V rewarded Vespucci for his many discoveries and named him pilot major of Spain. Vespucci spent the rest of his life teaching navigation. He taught new explorers the calculations he had used to determine latitude and longitude. In 1512, Vespucci died at home in Seville. As mapmakers drew new world maps, they used "America," the Latin word for Amerigo Vespucci's first name, to name the continents of North America and South America. It was a just **tribute** to the explorer Amerigo Vespucci.

Vespucci's Timeline

1451 Amerigo Vespucci is born around this time in Florence, Italy.

1483 Vespucci begins working for the Medici family.

1497 Vespucci's possible first voyage to what are now the southern and eastern coasts of the United States.

1501 Vespucci sails along the coast of South America.

1512 Vespucci dies in Seville, Spain.

Glossary

ambassador (am-BA-suh-der) An official representative of one country who visits another country.

astrolabe (AS-truh-layb) A tool used by navigators to measure the position of stars and planets.

circumference (ser-CUM-frents) The distance around something circular.

city-state (SIH-tee STAYT) A city ruled by its own government and no other.

constellations (kon-stuh-LAY-shunz) Groups of stars that have been given names.

continent (KON-tin-ent) One of the seven great masses of land on Earth.

equator (ih-KWAY-tur) An imaginary line around Earth that separates it into two parts, north and south. The area around the equator is always hot.

expedition (ek-spuh-DIH-shun) A trip for a special purpose such as scientific study.

hemisphere (HEM-uh sfeer) One half of the globe, usually the Northern Hemisphere or the Southern Hemisphere.

latitude (LA-tih-tood) Indicates position from north to south on the globe.

longitude (LAWN-jih-tood) Indicates position from east to west on the globe.

merchants (MUR-chints) People who buy and sell things for a living.

navigators (NAH-vuh-gay-torz) People who figure out which way a ship is headed.

pilot (PY-lit) To steer a ship.

quadrant (KWAH-drent) A tool used by navigators to measure the distance of stars and planets from the horizon.

rebelling (ruh-BEL-ling) Disobeying the people or country in charge.

trade route (TRAYD ROOT)   The path used to travel somewhere to buy and sell goods.

tribute (TRIB-yoot) A gift or message of thanks.

unified (YOO-nih-fyd) Two or more things that are brought together as one thing.

Index

A
Africa, 18, 21
Asia(n), 5, 9, 21

B
Brazil, 14

C
Cadiz, 9, 10
Columbus, Christopher, 9, 10, 13
continent, 21, 22

E
Europe, 5, 21

F
Ferdinand V (king of Spain), 13, 18, 22
Florence, Italy, 5, 6, 9, 11

H
Hispaniola, 13, 17

I
India, 9, 10, 14, 18
Indies, 9, 19

L
latitude, 14, 22
longitude, 14, 22

M
Manuel (king of Portugal), 18
map(s), 6, 10, 14, 19, 22
Medici(s), 6, 7, 9

N
Native Americans, 17, 21

navigator(s), 6, 10

P
Portugal, 18, 21

S
Seville, Spain, 9, 22
South America, 14, 21, 22
Spain, 9–11, 17, 18, 22

U
United States, 11

V
Venezuela, 14

Web Sites

Due to the changing nature of Internet links, PowerKids Press has developed an online list of Web sites related to the subject of this book. This site is updated regularly. Please use this link to access the list: www.powerkidslinks.com/famex/vespu/